Megalomaniac

SHAMSHAD KHAN was born in Leeds. She now lives and works in Manchester. She was introduced into the Manchester poetry scene through Commonword (writing development agency). Her first poems were published by their imprint Crocus. She has co-edited two anthologies of poetry for Crocus, including *Healing Strategies for Women at War*.

http://www.shamshadkhan.net
http://www.shamshadkhan.com

Megalomaniac

SHAMSHAD KHAN

CAMBRIDGE

PUBLISHED BY SALT PUBLISHING
PO Box 937, Great Wilbraham, Cambridge PDO CB21 5JX United Kingdom

© Shamshad Khan, 2007

The right of Shamshad Khan to be identified as the
author of this work has been asserted by her in accordance
with Section 77 of the Copyright, Designs and Patents Act 1988.

Salt Publishing 2007

Printed and bound in the United States of America by Lightning Source

Typeset in Swift 9.5 / 13

ISBN 978 1 84471 312 7 paperback

Salt Publishing Ltd gratefully acknowledges
the financial assistance of Arts Council England

1 3 5 7 9 8 6 4 2

for

jamsham

"I take one step towards you   you take one step back
I thought you didn't like me   you were just clearing the path"

Contents

Acknowledgements

Thanks and acknowledgement to all my family and friends, all my teachers and supporters including: Basil Clarke, Meeta Rani Jha, Prita Jha, Nicky, Shiela, Caryn Simonson and Lemn Sissay.

Apples and Snakes, Black Arts Alliance, Commonword/Culture Word, Live Art Development Agency, Spread the Word, The Contact Theatre, The Lychee Loungers, The Manchester Poetry Festival, The Arts Council of England and Arts Council, North West.

Bill Gee, commissioned "Body of Flowers" for Fragrant Gardens, Glasgow. Leeds Libraries/Word Arena residency supported initial work on "Hard Cut". Sitara Khan (my sister), her play "The Scented Fountain" inspired "Silver Threads". The Manchester Museum, Oxford Road commissioned "Pot".

The Green Room, Manchester, developed and launched "Hard Cut", "Honey" and "Megalomaniac", which were all directed by Mark Whitelaw.

A few of the poems in this collection have appeared in other publications: *The Fire People*, *Healing Strategies*, *Gargoyle*, *Redbeck Asian Anthology*, *Sable*, *Bittersweet*, *Velocity*, *Hair*.

Access Assured

in berlin symbols have meaning. things forbidden. arrows
guiding from dry land to water. water to cement. water squared
and tile trained. she could feel bone feet against ceramic
whiteness.

slipped from solid
to undulating screen   lotion of crescents. water shocked her
body. so she recognised it as hers. unfamiliarity ripped her chest
rib from rib. erected flag masts. not asking directions she ends up
in conversation. british flag buds sprouting. covering them with
her hands excusing. this is not a feasible explanation. the lower
ones touched sensitive show a greenness. tighten. she swims on
the green. unfolded moon slithers slipped like water from a leaf
and star drop. when she was smiling all her flags unfurled.

Camel Jaw

I burn myself in fires of perfection
dragged backwards through experience
I've unlearned what I need to

someone unravels my knitting

a board is wiped clean

my life's on the other side of a glass
you're not even looking my way

I was childish then

all those demands for attention

a foraging ant
where did the sugar cube go

it's in my hand
it's on my tongue

the ant is checking out
the lie of the land

I'm on the train
passing a splendid sky

I'm in bed
wake up suddenly

shocked at being alive

I feel water hit the insides of my chest
what me

I'm ecstatic
and daren't look back

then I'm frighteningly lonely

then human
kindness
ordinary

then breaking clouds
wow

I'm in a universe

giving up on old friends

anger loosening grip
letting go hands

I'm suffocating on air
you breathing out
behind me

your camel jaw
my hooves on sand

the sun is making my body cry
the way
only you could

the vibrating air
is eating you up

is that all you were

my skin coloured plaster
what I needed to heal

I'm pulling you off
slowly

slowly

I will have to rip the rest of you off

you take the top layer of my skin
with you

mushroom flesh
that has to forget

Black Elephants

jazz dancing

gold and red grin

I imagine they wave
as they pass
the window of my third floor flat
just in case they are
I wave back

Shatter Proof Glass

the nominations
for the urban music category
are:

a single white female
a short list of black male acts

they leave the girl to last
nothing unusual in that

black singers who can
behind
a white girl who can't
sing the blues
sings
'til the melody's been throttled
crucifying
your favourite song

and the winner is:

astounding

clasping her award
she's got so many people to thank
the record company
the producer
the manager
her mum
her dad
her gran
the taxi driver
all her friends

hopes she's not missed anyone
oh yes and

the backing band
god
couldn't have done it without you
the voting public
you being so
tone deaf
so undiscerning
discriminating

love you
need you
so much

we keep smiling
it would be mean nasty ungracious to
stop
clapping
when we hear

her crash through a
specially brought in
shatter proof glass ceiling

of the house of the music of black origin

Body of Flowers

lady slipper feet

meadow sweet ankles
delphinium legs
tiger lily thighs
rhododendron bum
rose hips
peony lips
mimosa balls
poppycock

gentian navel
wisteria waist
ivy spine
sunflower breasts
honey suckle nipples
daisy chain ribs

marigold shoulders

jasmine arms
buddleia biceps
pansy wrist
potted palms
foxglove fingers

buttercup throat
hyacinth chin
narcissus neck
chickory cheeks
mimulus mouth
tendril tongue
crocus nose
forget-me-knot eyes
snowdrop tears

daffodil ears
rose bay willow hair
vine mind
cerato skin

violet spleen
fuscia blood
lily liver
laburnum lungs
campion kidneys
lotus heart
angelica spit
comfrey bones

byrony bile
lavender shit
gladioli guts
dandelion piss

perennial spirit
clematis

Oppressed Coverage (1991)

It's not often you give us a prime time slot
but make an exception in times of trouble
when you star us on the news on ITV and BBC

bomb blasts it was us who did it
famines the result of Islamic rule
demonstrations only of mindless masses
women covered it's got to be oppressive

and it won't be the last time there's confusion
about Muslims and Islam in this nation
whether on radio or TV
rampaging fundo oppressive repressives
you know
even I'm starting to get
a negative picture of me

bomb blasts it was us who did it
famines the result of Islamic rule
demonstrations only of mindless masses
women covered it's got to be oppressive

and whatever the news
you restate your views with such ease
always finishing with a call to prayer
Allah-hu-Akbar

any excuse to show us on our knees.

When Do I   Do I   Do I Die

how long will it take. who will be there (do I know them now).
     do I like them/love them/hate them?
will I hate it. will I share it. will I care. will I want to die. will I
     remember everything that's ever happened to me.

where will I die (have I been there already) when will I first see
     the place where
I will die
will I know it when I see it

                    will I expire slowly or quickly.
                    will I gasp or rattle
                    have my eyes open or closed
                    will I be dressed or undressed
                    what will I be wearing
     what will I just have said
     who will I last have spoken to
     what will I just have eaten
     what will I have been expecting to do next?

will I have a lover
who of my family will still be alive. which of them will be talking
to the other. who will come and see me. will my hair be long or
short. will I have shaved my legs or armpits. will my feet be
together or apart. will I have shoes on. do I have those shoes now?
what will be the last thing I ever buy. the last book I ever read. the
last TV commercial I ever saw. will its annoying jingle be
bothering me when I am trying to die. who will I last have kissed
(passionately)? and have I kissed them yet. if my lover is not there.
who will tell them and how.

why do I die when I die. was there an alternative spot. more appropriate window

what toothpaste will I be using. will I still have tea with no sugar. will I be wearing glasses or contact lenses. will someone know to take my lenses out. or won't they bother. will I be on a period. what will be the last words I've ever written. will I have been to south america. will I still be with my current lover. will I wish I wasn't. what colour will I be in to wearing. when I'm dying will I know when it's finished or will it be like one of those plays where you don't know whether to clap until the house lights come on or are turned up and it starts with an apprehensive clatter

will I have enjoyed it. will I feel cheated will I just have got to grips with what it was all about. will I know how to die. will summers have got hotter?

Grids

Then the sun comes out

and where are you in all of this

grid coordinates
can you give me them

are you the pale chrysanthemum at 7f

or that heart-shaped world
squeezed between horizontal towers
two blocks away

if you could hold me in place like that
I'd love you for it

but I'm stencilled leaves
and runaway red squiggles

I'm the sliding rain
are you the window pane
or gravity

Classified

pull. pivot. tip.
withdraw weight
suddenly on the wrists
slide hands to balance push back in a bit.

there are thirteen of these.

the first you use all the time

the second pull out three inches. peer in.
the corner of a camera. a metal ruler. 2 cotton bobbins.
there is more
but you decide to
close.

telepathising over drawer three.
mind running checklists and answering.
no not that.
no not that
then
telephone directories. really out of date.
will throw them out
later.

drawer four. envelopes and paper
result of recent organising. 2 first class stamps

drawer five. still unopened packet of feathers. a few rolls of string
come off the reel and spaghettied. pens caught like fish.
deep sea rummaging. haven't seen this in a while [post card lover
sent from Japan
a lady on tip toe].
a stapler—it was here all the time.

should put it in the letter drawer. might find it easier next time.
drawer six. empty.
drawer seven. old post cards. birthday cards. valentines. sentimental
ribbon and packaging to be recycled.

drawer eight. cotton reels. big, small and medium. flat cardboard
sewing kits with
needles and either 12 or 5 options of thread colours. black thread
nearly run out on one. a flat silver thing with impressed pattern and
silver wire. no idea what it's got to do with sewing.

drawer nine. looks empty. a short pen advertising pharmaceuticals rolls
loudly as drawer opened and closed.

drawer ten. papers. cuttings from magazines. things you've forgotten
you did. odd sheets from newspapers. articles you can't remember
having read.

drawer eleven. photographs.
pull the whole drawer out and sit down. recent polaroid photo of four
people smiling.
picture of you and a tree.
picture of you and second youngest brother.
second youngest brother and three children taken about 2 years ago
picture of parents in back garden. looking young and healthy. taken
ages ago
picture of niece sitting alone.
picture of lover
who broke your heart. now fixed. doesn't crack when you look at him.
picture of sisters at your eighteenth.
picture of present lover smiling and cutting cake.
picture of you and previous lover taking picture of yourselves in
reflection in shop window . . .

drawer twelve. socks. new socks with cardboard stapled to the top. cotton rich. three pairs for the price of two.

drawer thirteen.

I've Been Waiting for Funding So Long

my performance idea
for a motorised miniskirt with automatic cold weather reflex
has had time to go out of fashion
and   come back in again.

The funding criteria seemed clear:
vision and imagination, quality of execution,
creativity of approach, capacity to encourage public involvement
        in art.

my application failed.
I tried again

they just loved the new proposal:
razzle dazzle tunic with pinstripe shalvaar
and union jack head scarf

cross cultural couture
positive action   sure to get a reaction
new audiences targeted and marketed.

next step the media.
very keen.

"the programming's no problem.
we've got the ideal slot
asian relationships and arranged marriages"

they like a hook
and usually find one size fits all.

I decide to risk it. Any publicity is   publicity.
we're on air.

"could you say a little about—
how you see the pinstripe "shall waar" as a symbolic
        representation of
post-colonial South Asia. a floating signifier rupturing cross
        cultural re-appropriation
of your cultural heritage"

I'm thinking about admitting
I was just taking the piss. but she's taken my pause
to conclude I'm not so quick.

she's already rephrasing "can I put it this way
if you were forced into an arranged marriage
would you be able to wear an outfit like the one you've created
or would this be totally unacceptable to your community".

Hard Cut

heard a heavy beat pound
felt the leaf fall
lighter snow fall
watched clouds drift
wondered   what drifting is

watched clouds drift   wondered
what drifting is
watched breathing in   wondered what breathing is
watched breathing out   wondered what breathing is

those flowers need throwing out
they're dead
somehow
sophia overlooks
the aubergine pale paper veins

a dried bouquet I'd planned to keep
at least a few more weeks
the sludge in the vase
alive as pond weed

above the water line
powdered white stalks
salt pins
secreted through the skin

the nurses were discrete
when my father stopped breathing
they left us time to contemplate
complete prayers
in other people's houses
it's hard to keep flowers
that extra day

without retching
I pull them out
black tongues of slime lick my fingers

I bend back the stems
the elbows splinter
where dry and wet meet

hold open the swing lid   push the heads in first
a green shoot
refuses to let the bin lid close
purple moth wings
slow dive to the lino

holding on becomes a habit to us all
pulling back a trigger
winding up the clock

not yet not yet
winding back the time
not yet
holding on   holding on to breath
watched
like a pot
with
the gas ring turned down
down
down
down
not yet
not yet

my brother watched
and watched
he went to get the nurse
when the simmering stopped

the nurse went to get the doctor
five minutes later
the doctor recorded the time
of death

two weeks of waiting
and waiting by the bedside
and some of us had missed the time

arrived at the hospital knowing something had passed

I'm ushered in
his youngest daughter
my father looks
a bit different
a bit stiller   a bit
calmer
than when he was snoring
I stand by the bed
recite the prayers he likes

the scientist in me
pulls out her pen and begins to chart
works backwards from the recorded time

to mark with precision
the exact point
the medical staff have been a bit slack

she titrates
drop by drop the heat as it leaves
the top of his skull
measured with control samples to ensure accuracy
drop by drop
changing night to day
slow dawning
my father is not dead did not die
I am not in denial
the words "he is dead" are not true
I will prove it

she extrapolates the continuous line
to find

the last breath
stretch and stretch
she has problems finding the end of it
the last trillion molecules breathed out
are still out there
glistening potential

my scientist splits seconds to find
where her father slipped out and someone brought in the
        replacement
there is no significant difference she concludes
between the before and after

the rest of me
prays his soul left
as easily as a hair
pulled from butter

holding on to who I think I am
fresh flowers at my father's feet
if he is not what I thought he was
then I can't be what I think I am
I get changed despite holding on

heard a heavy beat pound felt
the leaf fall
lighter snow fall
watched clouds drift
wondered   what drifting is

watched clouds drift   wondered
what drifting is
watched breathing in   wondered what breathing is
watched breathing out   wondered what breathing is

in the kitchen
my sisters grate carrot mountains
sunrise fingers
orange flecks in sugared milk
mother tests samples with her salt tooth
says
it's not quite ready yet
she turns the heat right down
by the time it gets to my dad
the alchemy is done

I should change. I've been wearing these clothes for days

the clothes in the wardrobe
are waiting for me
in between wearings the blue camouflage t-shirt inside out

the label showing washing instructions

getting dressed
I've tried to watch the transformation in the mirror
lose myself at the point of change
t-shirt over my head
the next thing

the seams are on the inside

single cell collapses
a black hair determined to turn grey
dead cells piling up on my scalp
powdered   powdered white death on my shoulders
I brush it off

not surprising I don't recognise my reflection
in glass panels
bus shelter screens
always in transition

abandoned houses
slow me down

ugliness gagged
at boarded-up windows

round the side
I search for beauty

slouched mattress
split white bin liner
horizontal daffodils
the garden's growing into a tip

an irresistible back door
I step in
drunk with darkness

the house pliant as someone asleep
poet and squatter
I do the decorating
plastering my dreams over
fading wallpaper

the air retains framed holograms of
nightmare disagreements
no answering back

impressed retinal image
grieving stars we're still seeing
after they're gone
bordering on knowing

don't look right now
I'm getting changed
no no go on
look   look really carefully

I've done it before
my father's done it before
last year about this time
they didn't think he'd make it

it was the same thing then waiting
for it to happen
not wanting it to
sometimes we didn't take our coats off or put our bags down
we got so much into it we forgot what we were waiting for
we saw it happen again and again

watched   breathing   in   watched
breathing   out

I go back into the room
hospital heat
and high dependency silence
dries my throat
my dad and half my family are in there
trying to put stars the size of pin pricks on to
3 millimetre spheres
the air pressure in the room making it difficult to breathe
minuscule feet hands the size of eyes
stained glass windows   purple robed prophets
slaughtered lambs   hanging from their bellies
a ship house   stench of cows
camels elephant's urine precious as nectar
sweat clams me to the chair

a camel comes over to me and starts telling me how it's ruined
        his life
he can't go out anymore
without being recognised
he gets hysterical I try to calm him down
push open a window
a hard rain of straws pour in at an angle
I shut the window and fasten the latch without getting wet
I'm preoccupied with trying to breathe

the camel is looking at the straws suspiciously
their orange light fills the room
a blue goddess with a bone cup drinking coffee
asks me if I take sugar
I tell her
I'm diabetic
she's already stirring

hands me a bowl of halva with no carrots in it
she goes off and returns as queen victoria wearing shalvaar
kameeze

someone opens the window
the camel has calmed down
my eyes let in more light than usual
I'm breathing more easily
repeating prayers I've heard

the first time I did it   I let myself off
then I did it again

I did the same thing bigger and better
the time after that I found I was shouting at myself
don't you ever learn and the next time I was shouting back
if you'd just give me a break and the next time
and the next time and the next time
and the next time I thought
is it that some things don't change
or that they do

every little mistake building up to the biggest bit of learning
every pause
a holding on about to let go

the camel looked at the straw suspiciously
it looked in many ways like all the other straws he had ever
carried
yet there was something that he didn't quite trust something in
the grain the glow of it

according to a recent survey of the top ten most overworked
animals

9 out of 10 are unable to distinguish the point when a load
        becomes dangerously heavy
the reports findings have serious implications for animal welfare
        in the area of safety at work
 a camel who participated in the research but didn't want to be
        named
said

"I was under pressure   I had deadlines to meet   I don't
        remember very much about what happened   And the
        worst thing is   if I ever saw that straw again   I'm not
        sure I'd recognise it"

excuse me
I'm trying to get changed

transition sounds like
undressing   undoing unfolding   smells like unearthing
unclouding   feels like unbending unfurling unknowing
        unravelling unrolling unsettling untying unwinding

a moment   swings itself
into being trapezing from before
to after

blood rush to the head
the momentum is the moment
in the split second it takes to split the second
it has happened
is about to happen and is happening
all at once

breathtaking

I train my eye on the swing and swing back
the throw and empty catch

building up momentum
till over the rung sequins and skin

catch myself in the morning
half awake
stagger forgotten how to walk

before breakfast
spoken to

forgotten how to talk

before I reconstruct myself
before I decide
out of habit
who and how I'm going to be
the clothes still in the wardrobe

there's been another death

the embalmer I set my tools
on the metal trolley
white sheets   camphor crystals
cream   water   cotton wool
small prayers to fill ears and other orifices

clatter of shoes in a heated hall
so many things to do and so many people doing them
including this one   doing dead

since my father died

I see everyone is dying
going in the same direction
as those who say they're living

exit routes and junctions noted
approximate time of arrival
a few leave early to avoid the traffic

heard a heavy beat pound
felt the leaf fall
lighter snow fall
watched clouds drift
wondered
what drifting is

watched clouds drift   wondered what drifting is
watched breathing in   wondered what breathing is
watched breathing out   wondered what breathing is

watched other things move or drift
this spring
I'll see the buds before they come
know the time before it is
hear light beat sound
feel the leaf fall
lighter snow fall
watch clouds drift   know what drifting is

every breathing in giving voice to the question
every breathing out the answer

watch breathing in   know what breathing is
watch breathing out   know what breathing is

this spring I'll see the buds know the time
before it is this spring

Back at Your Place

heart clasped like wanting

naked as the street—tears blown sideways across my cheeks
pulling my face tight
as they dry

park lamps dropping light like leaves

you were using the kitchen knife and black pepper grinder
so I left them

the shells were hazardous
too much of a reminder
of me

they were collected up in a jar
exposing the chipped white enamel
of the bath

your place would have looked too bare
without my plants

so I told them
—be strong

as soon as I'm settled
I'll come back for you

like a parent who isn't exactly lying
I promised
—I'll visit

months later
I come to collect plates
a pot I forgot

you look like family
you've grown new leaves

my fingers in damp soil
disappointed and relieved

Heart (Wrap)

I strap my heart
tightly
bind it strong

tough
was how I presented it to you

how you questioned me
on what was in this strange parcel

first tentatively
and then it in your hands
and feeling the warmth
and faint beat
you guessed

and since
have tugged at the string
I so carefully bound
in protection

how you teased open
layer after layer
unravelled it all
until it lay open before you

how you were repulsed
when you saw
the pale blood drained flesh

I too drew back

hardly recognising the half-healed mass
before us
disgusted by the scars
you did not ask
in what battle they were won

but fled

the faint-hearted
(I whispered to myself)

won't inherit

and began again
to bind

Simple Explanations

fairies reading from tiny books
fling out words that don't rhyme

grown women when combing their hair
will find the odd word
tangled there

Honey

1

she doesn't get cabs often

she prefers the anonymity of the bus

but when she does
it's usually late at night

it's parked up outside
headlights on

the driver's seen her at the window
so he doesn't blow the horn

she locks her door
and walks up to the car

like most single women
she's a bit wary of
getting into the back of a stranger's car
but she gets in and puts on her seatbelt

the driver slits the silence
with a question

kidar kay rehnay vaalayho?

then others that makes her even more nervous

shaadee hoi vi heh?
akaaylay rehthayho?

they're not pick up lines
though they could be mistaken for them

they're put down lines

lines put down like bait
see if she bites

this is not the usual cabby
and

she's not his usual
pick up

this line of questioning is
information gathering

from the slightest incline of the head
the subtlest tone

she decides how to reply

mostly she tells the truth out of habit
other times
she adds a little

"yes I'm married with three kids"

"no I'm separated my husband had an affair
with my sister so we can't ever get back together"

sometimes she feels like saying

yes I live alone

how about you?

when she's answering nearer the truth
she gives the names of the villages
her parents were originally from
then hopes the driver hasn't heard of them

Pakistan's a big place
England's a big place

but the world

is a small one

2

she's knocking on his door

it's late
he doesn't answer
so she uses the keys to get in
he'll be on the phone
in front of the telly
or making music

"how did you get here?"

she says "I got a taxi"
and leaves it at that

3

she's heard her mother say
she can't go through any of that again

so she hatches plots
all of them intricate

tightly planned
as a bee's dance

elaborate systems of communication
plots more complex than a
twister thriller

bluff
double bluff
double bluff and half it

she got used to keeping secrets
because an indiscretion
might cost someone an excommunication

telling quarter truths became a second nature for a while

when she started telling the whole truth again
she added something with it

to act as a decoy

4

sand on a beach

tide in and tide out

hard ridged sand under foot
and small in shore pools

head on his chest
as though she's listening for clues
hot sand
against her ear
her head
digging deeper

to be with him
ostriches in the sun
sand between their toes

and an unexplained fear

she has edged all her clothes with shells
smooth hard and grey
with serrated teeth like small shark heads
around the hem of her trousers   sleeves
around her neck line

a form of protection from guilt
and other things that might bite   or sting

they're watching TV

she's sitting on his settee
her special shell coat on and shoes off
just about to get comfortable

but looking as though she's on her way out

or paddling

years of acting like strangers in public
so as not to draw attention to themselves

they do it in private now
out of habit

5

he had no idea
she thought she was being watched for the first five years

they met up
but she didn't tell anyone for a while

it wasn't going to be easy

before he'd spoken she knew

a swarm of bees in her belly

warned her

6

nerves and lust had them bumping into each other all night

it was a relief to leave each other

just so they could walk straight

eventually he met her friends

she met a few of his
he met some of her family

she met some of his
nine years later

half their families
still missing to each other

she tried to explain:

"it feels like two timing

the way a nun married to god
might feel that she was two timing
on god
if she started seeing a man

they're like jealous lovers
asian families

they don't need to hire a private detective

to check if you're cheating on them

a bit like god they're omnipresent

they've got access to
just happened to be in the wrong place at the right time
asian aunty   informers

and if that fails the
asian taxi driver network"

they're not one of the numbers on her BT family
and friends list
but she knows the number by heart

sometimes she hears subliminal messages

the taxi radio anennae picking up

coded surveillance
calling all respectable asian households

co-ordinates
g9 e3 in the A–Z
young asian woman meeting with
man

he never heard the messages

7

his skin warm and welcoming
she gets hot just thinking about thinking about him

the sun catches the trees the trees catch the sun

the sun stops catching the trees
the sun light falls
dropped by the trees
it is morning

he makes great toast
the faintest layer of honey
like a memory

so she knows it tastes good
but she can't think
why

that many times
they met before

she mentioned

her family

might not approve

well probably would never approve

that she didn't really know what she would do

once he rang her at home

on her mobile

lucky she was sitting on the floor
on a chair and
she'd have fallen off it

his voice in her ear
at home

"are you alright
you sound a bit quiet"

exquisitely
ignorant

"work

someone from work"

she says it one too many times
"someone from work"

undercover lovers
thread thin
excuses

8

bees
lots of bees
nudging each other
nestling up to each other
pollen-tipped noses
and carpets
of honey

nothing too much trouble

liberating

to lose yourself in
selfless service

collecting   returning
making

swarm of love
co-operative
buzz

the hum at the table cloth
spread on the floor
continues

after the meal

no shoes
so there's no clatter

but
a lot of noise

children
honeycomb wax walls between them
tight squeeze
to fit back in

when they return
adults

a lot of noise

honey is thicker than blood
and love

is thicker than water

sweet clinging

sticking them in place

in the midst of the buzz
and the sound of the television turned down

her mother faces east
stands bends bows

stands
bends
bows

sits
and then
antennae crowned

picks up signals
of offspring astray

she comes to each of them
in turn
and prays

"let my children
follow the right path

let my children
follow the right path"

administering antidotes
sharp as a sting

"let my children not
follow the wrong path"

dirt   grit
stick

[48]

to their feet

they walk on honey

as they make to leave

   9

she's now   only ever so slightly paranoid

I'm not talking about black cabs
behind the slide back screen the big meter ticking in full eye view

no
the ones you ring up from home

she keeps her eye on him from the back
nylon fake fur car seat

stick on peel off
arabic script

multicolour sheen
on the dash

and a tell tale
thasbee
strung up around the rear-view mirror
she fingers the beads under her breath

his eyes flit
questions asked or masked

answered or carefully swerved to avoid head on
collision

in the back seat overly quiet

he gets a full view of her

she gives the name of the street

he sets off without saying anything

you see
he knows she knows he knows
that someone wouldn't approve

he takes short cuts "if you slow
down now it's about . . .
here"

he over hits the mark

by three car lengths
just where she wants it

a safe distance away

she's rummaging for the exact change

she has to ask him if he can change a ten pound note

he flicks on the over head light
turns
round
in his seat

she can see his face
lit from above

he can see her in the unflattering lights
at the end of a club night

she wishes she'd had the right change

they exchange money between the car seats

it's different if they ask right out

"you have a boyfriend?"

as though she's going to say yes

indignant as if he's asked her
does she do blow jobs
for money

"no"
tell a lie and half it

"yes
two"

tell a truth and double it

"yes

yes"
she practices saying yes

she practices telling the truth
it sounds more like a lie each time

10

relationships at the best of times
can create
tensions

misunderstanding
the central mode
of communication

but this is
all of that
with the little added pressure

of different cultures

and no family around to explain things

first you see fine hair line
fractures

nothing serious
those are easily covered over

then

there's a crack too wide
to fill

subsidence

the whole thing's about to cave in

that was how it happened

but

the first time they broke up
she said the reason was:

unsatisfactory time keeping

the second time
the reason:
honey
she knew she wasn't being reasonable

but there just wasn't enough of it
and he knew how much she liked it
how desperately she needed it to feel right

the third time
the reason:
too much
honey

it made her go funny
all that honey

the fourth time:
he just didn't seem to be trying
cold turkey
skin pricking
shivering

she kept trying to give him up

and each time they made up
the same old reason:

she gave in

warmed with
a voice
that
said
"things are simple

you want to see me
come round

'course come round
see you in a bit"

no complicated
honeycomb

of networked
reasons

just simple

come
stack up on me
sexy belly finger
slide yellow careering
honey
all over
golden

the odds were stacked up
against them

they knew they were
but
she'd got herself out of sticky situations before

but then she'd wanted to leave
now she's not really sure

like any addiction

11

this is well past the seventh time
and this time
it was him
who cracked
called it off

the phone hasn't rung

the mobile has no
"missed call" sign
hope breathes shallow

she may have done it this time

then the phone rings

the one hello she wants to hear

is the hello she said she didn't

though he hasn't spoken
she recognises him

even his silences
are special

12

they get back together

she tells him:
"you'll have to be worth everything I'll lose"

that
they'll have to have a plan

she comes up with a few

ways of introducing him
to her family
gradually

she thought she might try:

"he's the
 muslim friend
of a friend
of my best friend's brother"
or

"he was brought up muslim
got separated from his family at birth
and now
doesn't know anything about islam

but he's really willing to learn

and

that's how we met

he was looking at some islamic
books in a specialist bookshop

and asked me for some help"

she suggests

"maybe you could learn to say—

asalaamalaickum—

in case we ever bump into my family
unexpectedly"

"look"
he says

"it's simple

you want to be with me
and I want to be with you
you should just say that"

she thinks of jackanory and
play school nursery rhymes

13

7 honey bees sitting on the wall
and if one honey bee should accidentally
fall

there'd be 6 honey bees sitting on the wall

6 honey bees sitting on the wall
and if one honey bee should
accidentally try and fall . . .

there'd be 5 honey bees sitting on the wall

5 honey bees sitting on the wall and if

when it gets to her sitting on the wall
she just keeps sitting on the wall

and if
and if

and if one honey bee
should
there'd be . . .

consequences

because of this that because of that the other
and so it seems safer not to
act

14

select a pebble
or a stone that represents your partner

and another that represents you

and one for your family

can you place them in relation to each other?
do you see a pattern?

what happens if you remove the family?
how does it feel?

if you remove your partner
how does it feel?

remove yourself

how does your family next to your partner feel?

which stone feels best next to you?

which stone makes you happier?

15

over the years she has given away small clues

22 and still single
32 and still single
34 and still single
36 and still
no apparent
interest in boys   or girls

and no one seems to have guessed

she believes it's
down to her formula

tried and tested

it has been known to deflect even
the most persistent taxi driver
or

mi5 aunty
undercover informer

it goes like this:

if you're asked an awkward question
like:
"how come you're still single?"

you think of a lie
then half it
if you have to

tell the truth
but don't tell it to the first person who asks you
ask them not to tell three people
remember the first lie you told
multiply it by
nine

and take away
half of the truth

then finish with a categorical
statement of denial

so for example:

if someone asked if this story
was about her life

she'd say:

"no
not really"

then she'd say
"yes" (depending on who asked)
"but don't tell x, y or z"
then she'd say: "no, no . . . no" (nine times) "it definitely isn't

not really"

(then the final statement)
"this story does not relate
to my life
or that of any other asian girl or woman
not now not ever"

it works every time

Isosceles

you were obvious targets

shaven heads
with big fat black beards

bang
a flash of orange
a bloody shoulder

you heard your mother
break london's 4 a.m. silence
through the sounds of your own shouts
and theirs to

shut the fuck up
shut the fuck up
confusion

at the press conference
you said your head bounced down the stairs
when they dragged you by the foot

heavy handed incompetence
asymmetric warfare
this wobbly triangle

bush and blair and the rest of us
teetering

(Police raid in Forrest Gate, London of a Muslim family home. 15 police
officers entered their home unannounced, the remaining 235 stayed in the
street. One of the two brothers arrested, Mohammed Abdulkahar was shot
without warning. Both brothers were released without charge. The
investigation (June 06) did not charge the policeman, the shooting was
classed as a mistake.

Mat

any amount of piano tinkling key jangling crashing crushing
white teeth of ivory
black coal
won't rid you of this.
pain.
any amount of blue notes bobbing scaling insistent stepping,
stamping on the same spot.
running to a high place and jumping.
won't get you out of this.

this ....is.....
this is............ this..... is....... is....... is................is. this is.....
        where..... you..... have to.......
have to......... have to just stop.

stop being blue.
bend true to the words. bend bow true to the voice that's been
singing quietly three years now.
been humming low. lingering. nearly lost words to your soul.
saying stop. stop.

no amount of key crashing crushing jumping on the same spot.
rumplestiltskin mad angry deep wood mood in a
thought this was a secret place where no one else has ever been.

no amount of key jangling crashing will get you out of this. this
is the same place others have been. no new found territory to dig
in your heels.

this is a free to come. free to go kind of place. and if you don't see
anyone here with you now. they're watching. if you don't see
footsteps stamped before you. it's because

like cats pissing they cover where they've been. blue as a dog who
can't find his bone.
didn't want to leave any telltale marks because
you won't want to return to this place if you've ever been.

I Am Impatient

to dive into bed
with people
who know where fingers
and words are best put

and where not

I have stripped and walk out cold
for anyone who understands my nakedness

sees the spirit dress
of silent threads

and sees me dressed
and warm

I am a net of flies and wanting

I could not bar the way
to any cave

my thirsty tongue
licks the moisture
from your eyes

we speak with the same tongue
you and I

I keep my eyes closed
all the time

foraging   exploring

what I do not wear
you hold in your hands

and everywhere
that is not dry

is wet
and your searching tongue

has only to look

Megalomaniac

1

big wheels
small cogs

the machine is an illusion

unscrew the back
we are as interdependent
as those jagged teeth

however big or small

egos
all need oiling

I read books on egoless being
erasing the self
dismantling the contraption

trying for perfection
levels, planes, stations

just beyond my comprehension

one massive machine
I am told the body is an illusion
there is no head
there are no feet

one day there will be an
empty street
with an empty house
with an empty place
where my ego used to be

I'll wake as though from a dream
see things in a new light

birds flying into my eyes
and out of them

gold-leafed starlings
circling above me

I will place crowns
on everyone who speaks

the crowns dissolve
the people and their heads dissolve

rippling of the atmosphere

I become the object of all my desires
I become the thing that I want

tingling where my arms and legs
used to be
hairs standing on end

words reach my heart before they reach my ears
conversations with the moon

deep set ruby bursts into flame
smoke filling my empty room

I am vacating empty name
I am vacating empty name
I am vacating empty name

2

I put my scarf on
round the corner from the mosque

there's lots of rules
don't do that
do that like this

I know god is probably watching me
but I think he doesn't really mind

anyway some of what they say about
god definitely isn't true

in assembly mr cole tells us stories about being good
and how jesus was a kind person and jesus was the son of god

I like the stories but I think some of them have been made up
I know jesus can't be the son of god
because

at home everyone says
god has no mother or father so he can't have a son

and I don't think god would let his son die on a cross if he really
          loved him

but maybe jesus was naughty
people who love you have to tell you off if you're naughty

like mr cole
he's really kind but if someone is naughty
they have to go to mr cole's office
and he has to give them the ruler

the slipper
or the cane

put your hand out
nice and flat

whack
I make sure I'm not naughty

after primary it was junior   then middle then high school

in high school they didn't bother with the cane
they just had the bell

the bell
you run to your next class
walk don't run
the bell

telling you what to do where and when
the bell
period 4   science block   biology
conditioned reflexes

pavlov had a dog
every time he rang a bell he gave it food

then he would just ring the bell
and the dog would have his tongue hanging out
saliva dripping off it
expecting food
even if there wasn't any
it's a sort of training

classical conditioning
it's how we learn how to behave
an alternative to the carrot or the stick

the bell
I wait for teacher to say put your books away
the bell
it's time for the last lesson

I musn't be late
or make mistakes
if I get things wrong
I won't get on

3

we're in bed nibbling each others ears
we rule each other with feather fists
to avoid bruises and bust lips

you've built up a thirst
say you could do with a drink

backed up against the duvet
I try to assert myself

if you'd have asked
I would have consented

but as soon as it's expected
the conditioned reflex
kicks in

knee jerk
without thinking
I refuse

go on
get me a drink

demands disguised as requests
so we don't have to resort to the stick

you dangle another carrot
tell me power trickles down
if you compromise

I take a bite
it's sweet

I go fill the glass
rethink my tactics
on the way back up the stairs

stick your tongue out please
and say thank you

sex and money
can bring down a government

something trivial
like
who made the last drinks
can break up a perfectly good relationship

we play each others games
we give in
to get our own way

I learn to concede
you learn to say please
you say please
and I say thank you

I flex my love muscles
you try win me over with a kiss and a cuddle
no struggle

you crack the whip
I jump
you say
higher
higher please

we hold each others hands out
nice and flat

it strikes me
for someone to take power off me
I have to give it

4

I'm sitting on top
I've just been given world power of creativity

knowledge

all knowledge
of all things creative
is generated by me
I am never in the dark

the scurrying of artists
below me
I can hear the delicious sound of tongues
licking my boots

omnipresent
omnipotent

I'm on every page
of every chapter
of every book

I walk out on to the balcony
there's cheering
banners with my name on
photocopied black and white pictures of me
repeated on placards
as far as I can see

I raise an arm
all I can hear

shamshad khan

shamshad khan

I wave
there's a roar

they all want to be near me
they want my presence
want my inspiration
won't go till I give then leave

I don't have to lift a finger
but when I do

they acquiesce
will do anything to please

I'm so high
the air is thin
depleted of oxygen

my skin
has a rosy glow

I'm in total control of poetry
I have a monopoly on all words and rhymes

wordsworth and keats had to keep
referring to me
a lesser known poet
Lemn
is on his knees
he's begging for a metaphor

I say okay Sissay

but only if you
put your hand out
nice and flat

and say
please

he's a miner deep digging for words
writing till he sweats
ink splattered like blood

another brother thinks his writing's improved
but he hasn't got a clue
the words he's uncovered aren't new
they're all my cast offs
second-hand stuff

but for him they'll more than do
after all he's just the scribe
it's me who's the muse of the muse

T. S. Eliot prayed to me for insight
I start dictating
he thinks he's creating

Audre Lorde, Jill Scott, Gil Scott, Sylvia plath
get ready made lines
the freedom to write the way I like

my greatest devotee
lover boy Rumi

the things some people will do for me
another poet takes up idolatry

and then there's all the others

take Einstein
that idea of his
it was mine

that funky formula
that space time thing
my idea

those wacky sunflowers Van Gogh painted
mine
he was prepared to go out of his mind to get those off me

but it's the rap poets who really go for it
what they will give up
for the baddest rhyme
the hippest hop flow

I tell them they can go
take a long jump
over a wide wall
practise rapping faster
come back in nine
I'm not ready

I need time
they wait

wait days

some of these guys Biggee   Eminem   Missy Elliott
hang around mine
for weeks   months   years in a long long line

it ready yet
no?
it's okay they say
we cool
because they know
my words are heavy
always worth the wait

and when they get them
they're so pleased
so proud
they kiss my ruby ring
want to do me things

next they want to know how to
make a dramatic entrance
how to kick their opponents into the wings

who the other big names they might get to meet, in time

I say
amigos
no one else you need to know
with one exception

bow
down low
as I make introductions
high five
or knuckle touch
I suspect you may have already met

yes you guessed
it's your one
your only
true true friend

let me introduce
your
ego

ego is the drum beat—that knocks the guitar riff out of joint

ego is the leg—that trips that friend
who tried to get ahead

ego is the grain of grit
that stops the cog that turns the wheel
that drives the pump
that makes the light
that lights the stage

that some one else is on

ego is the oil your right hand needs
to grease the joint
that signs the deal
that twists the knife
that ends the life

of your biggest rival

    5

this season brown is the new black
this season
Asian Muslims replace African Caribbeans as the most oppressed

society gives us a score

you're born with something
but nothing's static

where there's nature there's nurture
where's there's snakes there's ladders

you can add to your score

we've all got choices
just that some of us got more than others

Asian woman climbing the ladder
she's doing alright
but she has to step on someone's toes or someone's knuckles
if she's gonna get her foot on the next rung up

society's built like a big house of cards
new york city
two aces topple

and over here
the whole pack gets shuffled

some of us go out of fashion

this season we're not passive Asians
this season we're raving Muslims
potential terror threats
headquarters in the corner shop

back on the ladder

we're dealt a new hand
and we play to win what we can
'cos we all want the same thing
just that

your bling
might not look like my bling bling

but we all want to be dripping in something

books, gold chains or prayer beads

conspicuous wealth
over stretched limousine
a big fat chain with a fuck of bling

or conspicuous education
a stack of flashy titles and letters after your name
to show off all that learning

high on success
we want to forget
what it's like to be down at ground zero
the outsider
the one without

and we hold tight
because we know it's a sliding scale
no one's safe

we're all Black
brothers
when there's plenty

but when things are short
a Jew is a Jew
Black means African not Asian
and Asian doesn't mean Chinese

only so much room under an umbrella
when it's raining

Somali refugee in Jamaican domain
Bangla boy in a Pakistani terrain

Vietnamese in poor white district
they know they have to take their chances

then some no hoper reaches for a gun
because he reckons he's never gonna get what he wanted

morality says try on someone else's shoe

squeeze your toes in
empathise

but for the grace of god
it could be you in the gutter
you
just want to get away from the nutters
got your eye on those fake
designer trainers

gonna take another step up the ladder
say
see you laters

    6

I take my shoes off
and put them next to all the other empty shoes
girls and small boys all go into the back room
big boys in the front room

there's a door in the corner of the back room
that leads upstairs
that's where the molvi lives

he has got no furniture downstairs, just carpets

and long benches like the ones we have at school
so we can put our qaiday on them

we're all reading out loud

I like doing the reading best when I can read it in my head
in my head it sounds really calm
but we have to read out loud so the molvi can hear if we're
    reading it right
he knows the whole of the qur'an by heart
so he knows straight away if we get anything wrong

he's got big feet and he never wears socks
he walks up and down the lines checking on us

you know when it's your turn because he
presses your shoulder with his stick

if you read it right
he says shaabaash
and he's walks past

if it's not right
you just get a little tap

then you have to
repeat after him
to get it
perfect

ahh
baahh

ajaz is on his second try
we can hear him

even though we're all trying to keep reading

he gets it wrong
so he gets a small tap on the shoulder

born with power
till it gets tapped out of you
tap

he tries again
he gets it wrong again
tap
tap you don't say it like that

the boy next to him gets the giggles

ajaz gets another tap
the boy next to him starts laughing
he can't stop

we've all stopped reading
even the older boys in the next room
have gone quiet
the molvi's face is really red and brown
he hits the laughing boy, hard

whack

then the laughing boy is crying
it's really bad if a boy cries
I don't think anyone makes any more mistakes after that

the next day
we all come to mosque as usual
we read like angels

we feel like we're in heaven
because
when the molvi was in the other room

someone said
hide it
quick

and when the molvi came back
he couldn't find his find his stick

7

I've always wanted to make things fair
balance them up
even if I'm just watching a football game or tennis match
I support the losing side, everytime

at university issues of equality were really high on my agenda
I'd managed to scramble through
but a friend of mine hadn't

I was studying biology   investigating "displays of social
        dominance in animal family life"
my thesis involved work with marmosets
little tufty-eared south american monkeys
a bit like squirrels but cuter
they were kept in cages up on the seventh floor of the
        williamson building

I know it sounds dodgy
but my plan was to make changes
not to release the animals
they haven't got a chance of surviving

on brunswick street
I wanted to improve the quality of life of the lower ranking marmosets

first I observe them
small family units
the same old story
two king pins and the rest subordinate

marmosets mark their territories
like dogs
to show who's dominant
the dominant ones mark most frequently

I set up a conditioning programme to reverse the social order
give the under dogs a blast at the top

what I do
is reward the subordinate ones every time they scent mark
I don't just ring a bell
I give them a little bit of farley's rusk
every time they mark

by the end of the project
the subordinates are marking like crazy
rubbing themselves up against the wire mesh
looking up at me
waiting for the reward
because they've marked
I give them a bit of farley's
they mark again × 3

the balance of power is tipped

they're marking like they're the top dogs
loving it

teeth baring
tail lifting
flashing their balls
showing off their bits

temporary anarchy
whack   a dominant gets hit

I have a tinge of guilt
all I've done is
replace one top dog with another
I've created a new hierarchy
forced a regime change

and who am I to say whether this new order is any better than
        the old one

8

wrong
pathetic

I'm just lying there impaled to the bed
the day has barbs that hook me by the gullet I have to force
        myself to throw back the covers
drag my feet to the floor
my head is in thick air

I'm feeling sick
I don't think I can do this

not that, not that
maybe this

I choose something to go with my mood
I dress down
over long sleeves
crossed at the back

—straightjacketed
—ready
—on my way for an interview

to avoid disappointment
I imagine the worst
they probably didn't mean to shortlist me
spiral of negativity

it takes the pressure off, for a while

then I get nervous again
try focussing on my strengths
but get distracted by my weaknesses
move myself on to the job description

I could make a huge impact
on the local community

a panel of five
looking in my direction and nodding

I look down

shit there's nothing under my feet
I'm way off the ground

I'm Wile E. Cayote running in mid air

who am I fooling I can't do this
before I hit the ground
I have to admit
I'm a fraud
a phony
I bigged myself up too much in my cv
they shouldn't believe my referee

I go all garbled
queezy

sprawled on the floor, cartoon stars spinning round my head
my mouth is freewheeling

I own up
I'm not roadrunner
I'm just a pigeon
no
I'm chicken
headless chicken

I sabotage the possibility of success
jeopardise my own chances

I hold my hand out nice and flat
whack

I do it myself
I don't give anyone else the pleasure

caged up in my self constraints
I dread the thought of change
so scared of being rejected
I leave before anyone gets a chance to show me the door

9

you—will—like—this
you—will—like—this
you—will—like—this

power is—what I want
ego makes—power

power is—ego

you will like—what I want

I am—what I want
I am—ego

you will like—power
you will like—ego

I am—what ego—makes
power is—what—I am

ego makes me—power

I am—the greatest
you will like—what I want
ego makes me

power is—good

10

shamshad says
kneel down
five times

shamshad says
turn your head to the left and
then to the right

ultimate control

god and me
got you on your knees

cross your heart
and hope to write a good line

shamshad says
bow down
shamshad says
lie down

turn over
ahh
got you

shamshad says
turn over

shamshad says take a pen in your left hand and try write a rhyme

I pull strings

I control my puppets
I give them what they need
they're grateful

I take it away
they try to stay hopeful

they follow all my instructions
they play the game
I change the rules
you have to climb up snakes
and slide down ladders

they excuse my whims
explain away their suffering

they believe   in a higher good to come
so they pamper me
repeat my name like it's a mantra

we   don't really need it
me or god

but it's kinda nice all the same

I guess even god could get hooked on all the attention
all those thousands of prayers and millions of pilgrims

me I've got artists gathered around me
like I was the black stone of ka'aba

at my feet
massaging each of my toes

oiling every joint of my fingers
my arms

my legs
my spine
my neck
my head
then I say

you can start again

I am supple and slick

quick
bring me my mirror
mirror
mirror

on my wall
ain't I just the cutest of them all
the most inspiring

ain't I the best
better than all the rest

11

my brother ajaz
was always getting in trouble
the naughtier he gets
the more he gets told off

the more he gets told off
the less he cares

the less he cares
the naughtier he gets

the naughtier he gets
the gooder I get
because I don't want to get told off

I'm a good girl so I get a smile

I'm a really good girl so I get to choose what I want from the shop

I get silver stars for merit
gold star for achievement
kisses and cuddles for being good

I get good at being good
but it isn't fair
because the gooder I get
the naughtier my brother seems

I set the plates out
humpty-dumpty lilac leaves

three sycamore seeds for you
and three for me

one egg for you
and one for me

my brother is digging
at the other end of the waste ground
he isn't bothering me

I've got smiley face leaning against the wall
she can't sit up by herself because
her leg has got a split

she had to get rushed to dolly hospital because
someone was naughty
and pulled off her legs

ajaz has stopped digging

he comes over

brown legs, ankle socks
boots

he kicks smiley face so she falls over

sit up properly so you don't get a tummy ache
he does it again

you'll get in trouble
if someone sees you

he kicks her again
and walks off

he goes back to digging

I collect all the plates up
put smiley face in my basket

hey have you seen this
ajaz is coming towards me

I start running
he's got a worm
hanging on a stick

he's running after me
I get to the end of the street

he's stopped four houses away
the worm's fallen off

he's crouched down
it might be a trap

I walk back

the worm is lying on the pavement
a streak of mud is coming out of its bottom

I dare you to touch it
no

urgh
he prods it with his finger
then picks it up and
waves it at me

I know what's coming
he's going to feed me for dinner
you know   if you cut it in half
it will make two

I know it's mean
but I suppose I say it so he will be on my side
and the worm will be on the other

anyway my brother goes in and gets a knife
he gets the one with a round end like that
that says sheffield steel

we both crouch down
we lie the worm out flat on the pavement

to stop it wriggling
I hold down the head and he holds the tail

you have to chop it there
in the middle

I think he didn't cut it right
because after that
the worm didn't move or even wiggle

we were going to bury it
but my sister comes out to get us for dinner

when she sees the worm she goes mad

I try to tell her it wasn't just ajaz's fault
but she doesn't listen

she already knows

ajaz is bad
and I am good

12

my ego is lying on top of yours
your ego is lying on top of mine
we are tumbling

naked flesh
human pyramid

one minute you're on top
the next it's me

active then passive
passive then active

you then me
bully
then victim
sadist and masochist rolled into one

we crack each others whips
jump higher and higher

ego boundaries blur

in bed
is where the ego
is most in danger

lying
on its back

sublime
momentary union
bodies blend
spirits converge
bliss

ego loses its identity

then one body is walking
away from the bed

subject and object split

is that my ego
leaving the room for a shower
or yours

ego remembers itself

[98]

it's yours

my ego sits up in shock
whilst your ego is showering

whilst my ego is getting out of bed
your ego is drying itself

whilst my ego is having a shower
your ego is getting dressed

whilst my ego is getting dried
your ego is feeding itself

and my ego is thinking of leaving

13

I'm feeling sick
is it something I've done
or something I've not done
didn't delete the right page
sent that text
to the wrong place

the day is wagging its finger at me
yanking my ear
telling me to hold my hand out

whack

I take a grip
I tighten control of the puppet
now I've got the job

I have to succeed in it
can't afford the price of failure

got to get myself out there
got to get things done
got to have things done good
got to have them perfect

I have to win
I have to take responsibility for everything

it's not safe to delegate
now that I've got my bone china plates
I keep spinning and spinning them

can't trust anyone

keep spinning and spinning

I turn into a control freak
afraid of being mediocre
because second best
isn't good enough

unless you're a man
and not just any man
a white man

a middle class, able bodied, straight, white, man

which I'm not

I'm a plate-spinning, headless chicken
dressed in wide-shouldered suits
I learn to swagger

take regular looks at myself
in the full-length mirror
I think I look alright
I think I look like a good plate spinner

14

I have their attention
they listen for my words

I make them
happy
sad

hopeful

desperate
as it suits me
I have more control over their emotions than they have over
        their own

I can make them stifle a sneeze
desperate not to cough
in case they disturb my   flow

I have made a woman cry
and a man whimper

with just a few words I uttered

my diction is perfection
my reticence magnificent

I put one

word in front of the other they
follow

I pause
they allow themselves to swallow

I drop a few lines for their pleasure
my audience makes me a coat of seamless applause

I'm not bothered by reviews from the critics
praise or blame it's all the same
when I'm wearing my tailor made suit of fan mail

I'm the, lead story, centre spread
even kicked the football off the back page

fans wanting my autograph
I sign my name
I sign my name
I sign my name
till my signature's just a squiggle

I'm in danger of repetitive strain
from all the waving
and handshaking
from all the adulation and praising
from all the beck and flipping calling
shamshad khan
shamshad khan

I make an exit from the back door
avoid the hordes and mauling

15

ego is sitting
on her throne
she is about to place the crown
on her own head

to reach freedom
we've suffered bondage

trapped in the cage of desire
bound by the mind

humiliated by need
internal compass spinning
disorientated

the machine about to break down

I take seven steps
each one a death
speeding past stations

on track for the goal I set
before I could reason
I am
therefore
I want
therefore I need

fingers disturb the water of reality
outward ripples

seven times the illusion is created and broken
another step taken

and within each seventh step there are seven more
and within each seventh another seven

there are books that say don't despair

nothing to lose
nothing to gain
absolutely nothing to protect

my ego feigns death
anything to stay ahead

I don't need
therefore
I don't want
therefore
I am not

I think I've got it hooked
it slips out of it's skin

I don't see the snake
just the rustling grass

I, I, I
the machine gets jammed

my head overheats
a row of sprinklers is set off

rain pours down the inside of my skull
collects in my eyes

drips down

onto the seventh illusion

a four   chambered   muscle

contracts and expands
contracts and expands

contracts and expands

It Looks Like a Map of the World

it looks like a map of the world
but it's the map of an angel
in reverse

tulips and thistles

he has no face
just flower prints

she is red
possibly dead

but the world is green

traces of bodies
open invitations

An Alternative to Plastination

each ant
will carry one single black hair
each

eyebrow
eye lash
nose bristle

moustache
goatie whisker
bum fluff
pubic hair
big toe tuft

then there will be a ceremonial line dance
as the ants

follow a detailed body map
build
a hair and air effigy

replica
of you

and if we were still in love

I would arrange
to have a few stray hairs
of mine

woven in between the spaces
that would be you

Ms Havisham

His was a deep red, sweet blood
sticky kind of love

that damned spot
oceans could not erase.

I stagger light headed
towards the crimson screen
where Ms Havisham still sits and waits

her wedding dress grey with dust
her friends not yet arrived.

The groom she has resurrected
at the head of the table

lover's banquet
candles flickering light and shadow
on her expectant face.

Her yellowed skin hangs
dull half opened eyes
peer across the table's lace landscape.

Cobwebs the spiders have deserted
drape the untouched feast

the carcass of a pig
long dead
skeleton tent
vacated shelter.

She bears no mind to the new life emerging
pink unopened eyes bulge

warm thin flesh around pea hard bellies
doesn't hear the high-pitched squeals of mice

but smiles
red lip stick lips politely

and passes the wine
to her hungry ghost guests.

On Understanding Our Dragons

There was a deep down place where her monster
rested on good days
quietly   only the flicker of a tail or eye lid
on good days   she basked
with her foot rested on her monster's back
her left cheek against its right cheek
her head slightly upward tilted.

on good days   she could come out   and be out
and her monster would still lie   only stretching its legs
repositioning its tail or the direction of its yellow ears

today was a bad day.
dream drugged and overrun with anxious anger
she was wilding in the storm of her dragon
opening her mouth and crying why why why

her monsterdragon was thrashing its tail   its eyes open wide
         open and red   flared at her
cursed her   twisting inside of her   blowing fire breath
out of her
when she closed down   stayed in   laid low
it blew harder

today was
a pretty bad day.
when she finally went out   met with friends
she said the wrong things
upset their monsters
so they red-eyed flared at her
lashed their tails and claws at her   from inside
her monsterdragon raged
the more she apologised
the more   they raged

today   was the very worst day.
when even at the end of the day she returned home
talked to her monsterdragon quietly on the way
reassured it there wasn't a dispute   that it could be resolved
that tomorrow she could rest her feet on its back again
and the next day   hold her left cheek against its right cheek
reassured herself and it   that other monsters were worse than hers.
today they both knew   she didn't believe it anymore

Pot

so big—they said you shouldn't really be moved

so fragile you might break

you could be from anywhere pot

styles have travelled just like terracotta
you could almost be an english pot

but I know you're not.

I know half of the story pot
of where you come from
of how you got here

but I need you to tell me the rest pot

tell me

did they say you were bought pot
a looters deal done
the whole lot
sold to the gentleman in the grey hat

or
did they say you were lost pot
finders are keepers you know pot

or
did they say they didn't notice you pot
must have slipped onto the white sailing yacht

bound for england.

someone

somewhere

will have missed you pot
gone out looking for you pot
because
someone
somewhere
made you
fingernails
pressed
snake patterned you pot
washed you pot
used you pot
loved you pot

if I could shatter this glass
I would take you back myself pot.

you think they wouldn't recognise you pot

say diaspora
you left now
you're not really one of us.

pot I've been back to where my family's from
they were happy
to see me
laughed a lot
said I was more asian than the asians pot
I was pot

imagine.
the hot sun on your back

feel flies settle on your skin

warm grain poured inside

empty pot
growl if you hear me

pot?

pot?

Dedicated to a Nigerian pot currently incarcerated in the Manchester
Museum without charge or access to legal representation.

Silver Threads

Together we built a palace
mahal   domes and minarets
tiny blue tiles and mirrors

wandered hand in hand
warm feet   on cool floors

ran up stairs to call from towers piercing skies

rushed through gardens
pomegranates and white flowers
ruby sweet pungent scent

trailed feet in fountained water
and when night fell   argued how many stars
embroidered the sky
sari like folds from the heavens to drape us
liquid blue chiffon and silver threads
we lay and unthreaded

how rich we were   silver knots
untied piled high

it was whilst I was lying
stars in my hands and the heavens on my lap
that you left.
I searched amongst the reams of translucent hope
fearing at first   that you had been smothered

or like a baby
choked on a silver thing

I searched our palace for years
until no longer ours   it became mine

all hope lost
single voice ringing
echoes returned   thrown from wall to
wall

I gathered our treasures and hid them in my purse
silver bits   spangled love

proof that I had not dreamed alone.

Printed in the United Kingdom by
Lightning Source UK Ltd., Milton Keynes
137579UK00001B/223-240/A